MW01227324

The real history

of

(Clan) Gunn

3rd edition

by

Alastair Gunn

the Gunns ... (are) a branch of the purest aborigines of the north[1]

the Gunns ... from the far north of Scotland, are descended from Pictish tribes...[2]

This booklet is a print on demand text; it is possible that new information could be found which means I might produce a further edition.

See http://www.lulu.com/spotlight/awgunn or https://www.facebook.com/ClanGunn1 for possible further information.

---

[1] Page 173, Thomas Smibert, *The Clans of the Highlands of Scotland.*
[2] Page 64, Gilbert Summers, *Traditions of Scotland.*

Contents

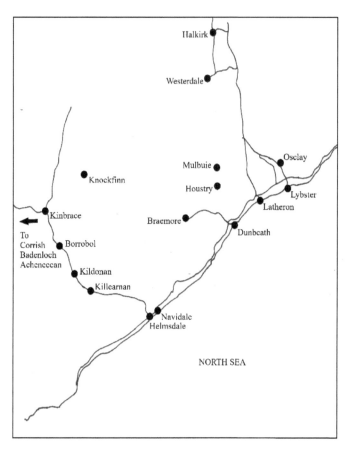

Some key places in Gunn history near Helmsdale,
north Scotland.

Introduction

I have recently written a detailed, fully referenced book called *The Gunns: History, Myths and Genealogy.*

This booklet is a simplified version of that text; my evidence for many comments in this book can be found in the larger one.

The reason I wrote the big book is that so much traditional Clan Gunn history is a load of codswallop. Yes, what currently masquerades as Clan Gunn history is essentially nothing more than a mix of fiction, mythology and half-truths.

Gunn history is really simple. Gunns were the earliest, mainly non-related inhabitants of northern mainland Scotland. They are not a Clan on any historic or academic basis as Clans need a founding father and Gunns do not have this. The supposed, historic Clan Gunn Chiefs do not stand up to scrutiny.

'Clan' Gunn is an invention which started in the early 1800s and which has developed over time.

The first known Gunn in history was Coroner Gunn of Caithness and he died in about 1452. His senior descent line is the MacHamish family group. The senior MacHamish line has not died out and some have continuously held the surname Gunn since Coroner Gunn's time, including my family line. This is the Clan Gunn Chief line.

June 2023

Kildonan 2011

1. Origin and meaning of the surname Gunn

The Gunn surname is by origin a regional surname as the Gunns were the original, but not consistently related inhabitants of northern, mainland Scotland.

Ptolemy, in the second century, records the names of the tribes of northern Caithness and Sutherland as Cornavii, Caerini, Carnonacae and Creones / Cerones. That's viewed as too close a set of names – it is probable that they were all one tribe.

The spelling of these names was not fixed so by 1836 these tribes are all recorded as Kournavii – Kourns, if you like. We have no idea what the name Kourn meant but over time the word evolved into Gunn (or more accurately Guin as this was the earliest known signature used by a Gunn in August 1638). These early Kourns / Gunns lived inland from the coast of Sutherland and Caithness, an area not conquered by the Norse.

The Gaelic / Celtic / Erse meanings of the word Gunn are terms like fierce, sting and wound. So, Gunn is a group noun meaning, in effect, 'nasty people - avoid' and was used about the inland Gunns by those who lived in the settled coastal areas controlled by the Norse from around the 800s and for some centuries afterwards.

We have no idea what the Gunns called themselves. We also have no idea what the Picts or the Caits of Caithness called themselves. That does not matter. The name Gunn stuck to the people of inland northern mainland Scotland.

The noted author Ian Grimble[3] wrote

A typically mysterious tribe of the far north is the one called Gunn ... The Gunns inhabited the mountainous area which contains Morven and the Scarabens (being the mountainous area of modern Caithness). *To the south the hills descend to a level plain along the Moray Firth, which provided the Norsemen with their accessible Sutherland. But north of the Helmsdale river the east coast consists of huge cliffs, as intimidating as the hill country behind them. The entire area is rich in pre-historic remains, proto-Pictish defensive structures and later Pictish sculpture ... it was exactly the sort of refuge that the old inhabitants were likely to have chosen when invaders arrived ...* (the name) *Gunn might be so old that it belongs to a pre-Celtic language ... What seems most likely is that the Gunns were a Pictish tribe.*

Summary

The name Gunn is by origin that of a regional, non-related tribal group of northern Scotland.

---

[3] I thank Sir Charles Fraser for pointing out this comment from page 64, G. J. Summers, *Traditions of Scotland.*

2. Why Gunns are not a traditional Clan and have no Orkney Islands Clan Gunn Chief links

As said, Gunn is by origin a regional name for a non-related tribal group of original settlers of northern mainland Scotland, in other words Gunns had no founding father. This means Gunns are not a traditional Clan as such Clans must have a founder.

Nor were there any historic Clan Gunn Chiefs.[4] There have, however, been many fantastic stories over the years about these supposed Chiefs.

One idea involved Gunn Chief descent from Guðrøðr who was a son of Olave the Black, King of the Isle of Man. Another involved descent from Gunni, the brother of the great Orkney pirate Sweyne Asleifsson. Neither of these stories lasted.

The current myth involving Clan Gunn Chiefs starts with the Orkney Islands and descent from Gunni Andresson - the supposed initial Clan Gunn Chief - who was born around 1180. There are insurmountable problems attached to this fantasy.

Firstly, there is the problem of the fixed surname Gunn. Highlands and Islands surnames were not fixed until the 1700s. It was all Scandinavian 'change surnames every generation' until the 1700s – for example, **Gunni** Andresson had a son called Snaekoll **Gunnison**. Note

---

[1] A Clan Gunn Chief was invented in 2015 by Lord Lyon but this is legally questionable as Lord Lyon did not follow the stated practice of his Court at that time and even more importantly the Supreme Court of Scotland - the Court of Session - has ruled that Lord Lyon does not have the power to appoint Clan Chiefs.

how the first name of the earlier generation became the surname of the second.

Those who believe in the Clan Gunn Chief Orkney Islands origin idea have to explain how the Gunn surname became fixed hundreds of years before everyone else's in the Highlands. That's not possible. Gunn as a regional name applied to those living in an area solves that problem.

And why would the Gunns be named after Gunni Andresson who was basically anonymous in history? All he did was marry well. People who start Clans are famous and did things. Gunni's grandfather was the well-known pirate Sweyne Asleifsson – think 'Pirates of the Caribbean' – and he is in all the history books. If Gunns were now called Sweyneson (Swanson) then that would have been logical, ignoring the previous paragraph about no fixed surnames.

The next problem concerns the aristocratic, nasty Snaekoll Gunnison[5] (1200 – 1239) who is the imagined second Clan Gunn Chief.

Snaekoll never married and never had children. In 1231 he was dragged, in disgrace, from the Orkney Islands to Norway and spent the rest of his life there after murdering Earl John who was the King of Norway's Governor of Caithness and the Orkney Islands. Snaekoll

---

[5] Snaekoll's life is documented in the *Orkneyinga Saga* and the Norwegian *Hákonar saga Hákonarsonar*. In neither of these texts is there mention of Snaekoll marrying, having children, nor being forgiven by the Norwegian King and so being able to go back to Scotland. And such events would be in the texts as Snaekoll was too well known to be ignored.

was jailed for some time fairly quickly after his arrival in Norway as the King was not impressed by Snaekoll killing the Earl. Snaekoll is last heard of leading rebels in a losing battle against the King. And the King was known for his ruthless repression of that rebellion...

Dr Barbara Crawford[6] is one of the key academics in this area and she has written that

Despite his part in the murder of the earl Snaekoll was not condemned to death at the trial in Bergen (Norway) *... and there is no evidence that he ever returned to Orkney or Caithness* (then, footnoted) *Despite the claims of Clan Gunn to be descended from him.*[7]

In other words, Snaekoll has no relevance to Gunn history.

The third problem with this supposed Clan Gunn Chief Orkney Islands descent is Snaekoll Gunnison's imaginary son Ottar Snaekollson. The fantasy Gunn history supporters like this Ottar as his existence 'proves' Snaekoll Gunnison made it back to Scotland and had a son.

---

[6] 'Dr Barbara Crawford M.A., Ph.D., F.R.S.E., F.S.A., F.S.A. Scot., Member of the Norwegian Academy ... Honorary Reader in History at the University of St. Andrews ... Dr. Crawford is a Member of the Norwegian Academy and a Fellow of the Royal Society of Edinburgh. She was a Commissioner of the Royal Commission on Ancient and Historical Monuments of Scotland from 1991-2001, chaired The Treasure Trove Advisory Panel for Scotland from 1993-2001, and was President of the Society of Antiquaries of Scotland from 2008-2011. She was awarded an OBE in 2011 for services to history and archaeology, and has recently been awarded an Honorary Professorship at the University of the Highlands and Islands...' from https://www.st-andrews.ac.uk/history/staff/barbaracrawford.html accessed 14 March 2016.
[7] http://research-repository.st-andrews.ac.uk/handle/10023/2723 accessed 14 March 2016; page 8.

It proves nothing of the sort as the Ottar Snaekollson in the history books was a Sudreyan Chief from the west coast of Scotland and had nothing to do with Snaekoll Gunnison.

The proof is simple. The Ottar Snaekollson who negotiated with the King of Norway did so in 1224. His supposed Gunn father Snaekoll Gunnison was, however, born around 1200 as Snaekoll's mother's first husband died in 1198. So, if Snaekoll had married and had a child then that child would be no more than four years old when dealing with the King of Norway which is obviously an absurd idea.

Gunni Andresson, Snaekoll Gunnison and Ottar Snaekollson all existed but none have anything to do with Gunn history.

Summary

Gunns are not a traditional clan as they had no founding father. There is not the slightest shred of evidence to support any Clan Gunn Chief descent from the Orkney Islands. Gunns can be considered a modern clan following the tartanisation of Scottish history due to the influence of Sir Walter Scott 1771 – 1832.

3. Fantasy 'Clan Gunn Chiefs'

The first supposed Clan Gunn Chiefs namely Gunni Andresson, Snaekoll Gunnison and Ottar Snaekollsson were at least living people although neither had anything to do with the Gunns. Of the fantasy Chiefs after them only one actually lived, and he was not a Gunn

*****

The most commonly accepted version of Clan Gunn Chiefs after Ottar Snaekollson is -

1. James de Gun
2. Ingram
3. Sir Donald Gun of Clyth and Ulbster *('of' means the person owned or rented the Estate; being 'in' a place means you just lived there)*
4. Sir James Gun of Clyth and Ulbster

But these names fail for variety of reasons –

- There is no historical proof to support James de Gun, Sir Donald Gun or Sir James Gun ever living.
- Ingram is just wrong – he lived but was a not-Gunn. This Ingram is really Enguerrand De Guines, Lord of Coucy.
- There is no link from one name to the other – as in 'his Mum and Dad were…'. The list is just disconnected names, not successive, linked Clan Gunn Chiefs.

- How on earth did James de Gunn get a Norman 'de' into a far north Scottish name and then where did it go? Normans were powerful – if 'de' had got into the Gunn name then 'de' it would have remained.
- There are two supposed Clan Gunn Chief knights to finish with, but Scotland did not have knights (except for Royalty and those Royalty related) in these early years. And given knighthoods were inherited why wasn't Coroner Gunn (discussed in the next chapter) a knight as knighthoods were inherited? The answer is simply that the knighted Gunns did not exist.
- And, again, why - and how - did these 'Chiefs' have the surname Gunn when all the other Highland Families still had changing surnames…

Summary

The supposed Clan Gunn Chiefs after the Orkney Islands people fail every test. They are not part of real Gunn history.

4. Coroner Gunn, the first Gunn in history

The Gunn who held the important position of Coroner of Caithness and who died in approximately 1452 is the first Gunn known in history.

There is a Gunn 'Westford Knight' story which says a Gunn helped explore America in 1380, which is earlier than Coroner Gunn, but the exploration the Gunn was supposedly on has been conclusively proved a hoax time and time again; the *Dictionary of Canadian Biography* calls it 'one of the most preposterous ... fabrications in the history of exploration.' The Gunn 'Westford Knight' fantasy should be relegated to the fiction section of the library.

We do not know the full name of Coroner Gunn but we obviously know his position. Coroner was a seriously important job at this time; each region of Scotland had at the top of the social and legal peak an Earl but in Caithness in Coroner Gunn's time the Earl was 'in abeyance' – no-one had it. The second in charge was the Sherriff but he lived and worked in Inverness in the Coroner's time. So, this left Coroner Gunn in charge of Caithness. It was not an inherited position.

Being a Scottish Coroner is not like the position today. A Coroner then was mainly about protecting the King's finances so the Coroner dealt with living criminals, confiscating property and was a sort of bailiff. The Coroner was also responsible for law and order so had quasi-military powers. The position was signified by wearing a great brooch, such a brooch has been attached to stories about Coroner Gunn. It was obviously a position of major responsibility.

Given the absent Earl it is probable that the Coroner lived in the Earl's Castle as part of the perks of the job. After all he needed somewhere to suit his important position, lock up criminals and somewhere to store the goods confiscated for the King. This castle was probably that of Sinclair Girnigoe. Coroner Gunn's 'Castle' was just part of the job – it is also the only logical reason why the family leaves the Castle after the Coroner's death.

As said, the Coroner died in about 1452. He died after some Caithness people killed him in an attack somewhere near the Church of St Tayres. These Caiths (not Keiths, the idea that Keiths and Gunns had a longstanding feud does not survive examination as the Keiths were one of the most important families of Scotland and the Gunns certainly weren't) probably got annoyed with the Coroner following a disagreement about going to jail, or the Coroner being too enthusiastic about confiscating property.

We do not know the name of the Coroner's parents (again an insurmountable problem for those claiming Gunn Chiefs descend from the Orkney Islands) nor the name of his wife. We do, though, have a range of suggestions for his children and these are often contradictory in name and sequence. The two main ones were firstly James Gunn of the Killernan Estate, the senior Gunn line. This family line is traced through the rest of this text. The second son was Robert Gunn of Braemore. His line can be traced; various minor myths and some involvement in the brawls of the time are known. For purposes of keeping this book short I have not covered those events here – readers interested in these events should see my larger book *The Gunns: History, Myths and Genealogy.*

5a. Senior MacHamish Gunns / 'Clan Gunn Chiefs' to William Mohr

The main Gunn history after the Coroner is with his senior descent line – the MacHamish Gunns, later called the Clan Gunn Chief line. As already discussed there were no historic Clan Gunn Chiefs, that idea was invented in the 1800s.

On MacHamish Gunns

The word MacHamish has been wrongly used in various Gunn 'history' books. MacHamish means 'son' of (more accurately 'descended from') James (Hamish), the senior son of the Coroner. In other words, MacHamish indicates a particular Gunn family group. Other Gunn family groups include Braemore Gunns and MacHeorish Gunns.

This sort of family group indication is quite common in Scottish Highland families. The reason for these indicators is simple – it helps clarify who you are talking about as more than one person can have the same name. This indicator was of importance in legal matters.

MacHamish does not mean 'Chief of the Clan Gunn' as some believe as if you were 'Chief of the Clan Gunn' then 'MacHamish' as a title would not have been needed. And as you could have two MacHamishes alive at the one time it was certainly not a title held by just one person. Two MacHamishes certainly happened – see the following lives of William Mhor Gunn and his uncle William Beag Gunn.

The Senior MacHamish line from Coroner Gunn to William Mhor

Throughout the rest of this book numbers such as the 8. before William Mhor indicates the generation from Coroner Gunn. The Coroner is generation 1. A new generation is needed about every thirty years or so given lack of modern birth control methods. Generations 3-5 are problematic. Names and number in bold show the senior ('Chief') descent from the Coroner such as for **8. William Mhor GUNN.** This bold is normally only used for lists or at the start of a biography. After the death of **11. William GUNN** the bold is shown on the Senior MacHamish Gunn descent line known in 2023. Various other senior Gunn lines have become extinct over time.

1. **Coroner GUNN** (d. c. 1450)
    2. **James GUNN** (c. 1420-)
        3. **William MacHamish Cattigh GUNN** (c. 1450-)
            4. **William MacHamish GUNN** (c. 1480-)
                5. **Unknown MacHamish GUNN** (c. 1510-)
                    6. **David GUNN** (c. 1530-)
                        7. **Alexander MacDavid GUNN** (c. 1560-c. 1624) Sp(ouse). Barbara MACKAY (c. 1570 -). *With brother 7. William Beag Gunn whose descendants become the Senior line. See Chapter 5b.*
                            8. **William Mhor GUNN** (c. 1593-) *Died without issue.*

Biographies of the Senior MacHamish Gunns to William Mhor

1. Coroner GUNN

Coroner GUNN died in about 1452. His life can be found in Chapter 4.

2. James GUNN

James GUNN was born around 1420. He was the eldest son of the Coroner. James is an anglicised version of his name and such anglicisation occurs for others in this book. James moved out of the Castle his father occupied which proves it was not a Gunn owned castle. Why would an eldest son leave a Castle which he would inherit?

James settled at Killernan – a farming estate - where he was a tenant of the extremely wealthy, massive landowning Sutherland family. It is not clear whether James moved out before or after his father's death. It is probable that other members of his family settled at Killernan with him; a large farm requires labour and can feed many people. It was certainly before the time of the nuclear family.

James may have died in 1487; he was an unremarkable character and no stories definitely exist about him. The lack of stories further shows that 'MacHamish' is nothing more than a family group indicator.

3. William MacHamish Cattigh GUNN

James's son was William MacHamish Cattigh GUNN who was obviously the first MacHamish and was born around 1450. He, also, is basically an invisible person.

Cattigh / Cattaig means a resident of Sutherland.

4. William MacHamish GUNN

It is probable that William MacHamish Cattigh GUNN had William MacHamish GUNN who was born around 1480.

There is record of a William MacHamish fighting at Torran Dubh in 1517. He was a subordinate leader and there is no mention of other Gunn involvement. It was very sensible to be involved in this battle –William was on the Sutherland family side from whom his Killernan Estate was rented. If you did not fight for your landlord - the establishment side - in this battle one can imagine the zero chance you had of holding on to your property.

This fighting William MacHamish could not be 3. William MacHamish Cattigh GUNN as that William was born around 1450 so would be too old to have fought in 1517 if he was still alive.

There is further record of a William MacHamish being alive in 1525 which is too late to apply to generation 3. William MacHamish Cattigh GUNN as people did not live long at this time. So, again, a generation 4 William MacHamish Gunn is needed.

This William MacHamish GUNN was probably the eldest son. He might not be. Other possibilities exist including that this William could easily be a fighting orientated younger brother whilst an invisible, unknown Senior MacHamish stayed at home on the farm.

5. Unknown MacHamish Gunn

William MacHamish GUNN had a son Unknown MacHamish around 1510.

This Unknown MacHamish GUNN is needed as there is record of a 'MacHamish Gunn of Killernan' fighting in 1542 at the battle of Aldi-Be-Beth, a 'MacHamish Gunn' fighting in a 1549 battle and a 'MacHamish Gunn of Killernan' fighting in 1556. None of these records provide a first name. The 'of' suggests it was the Senior MacHamish of Killernan doing the fighting as 'of' meant landowning or the person renting the land.

The MacHamish Gunn in these 1542-1556 battles cannot be 4. William MacHamish GUNN as he was born around 1480 and so would have probably been dead or, at the very least, totally incapable of engaging in this fighting.

There is no record of other Gunns being involved in any of this fighting; as often said the Gunns of Killernan were not Clan Chiefs who led Gunns.

6. David MacHamish GUNN

The Unknown MacHamish GUNN had David MacHamish GUNN who was born in the 1530s.

This David does not appear in the traditional line of Clan Gunn Chiefs but this David's elder son is clearly identified as Alexander MacDavid GUNN in Clan Mackay histories. See the next biography. With a MacDavid GUNN we, obviously, need a David GUNN as his father.

And the years work for David MacHamish GUNN. We have a MacHamish of Strathully in 1570 being a good friend of the young Earl of Sutherland. David MacHamish GUNN would have been around the right age for the friendship – his father would have been too old, if not dead.

David MacHamish GUNN also had a second son called William Beag GUNN (see Chapter 5b).

William Beag's descendants become the Senior MacHamish line after Alexander MacDavid GUNN's line ends with the death of Alexander's son William Mhor who did not have any known issue.

7. Alexander MacDavid GUNN

Alexander MacDavid GUNN married Barbara Mackay, a daughter from the second marriage of Iye Du Mackay of Farr, 12th of Strathnaver, Chief of Clan Mackay.

Barbara is important as she adds a definite date to Gunn history. Barbara's brother was Huistean (Hugh) Du Mackay 13th of Strathnaver who was the eldest son of his father's second marriage and all sorts of histories give his birth date as 1561. Barbara is listed as the fifth child of that second marriage; a birth year of about 1570 is therefore reasonable for her. This 1570 suggests a birth year of about 1560-1570 for Alexander MacDavid GUNN.

Barbara's birth date of 1570 provides a challenge to a Clan Gunn Chief myth which has her married to an invented generation 4 'Alexander MacHamish GUNN' – as already said, Barbara married generation 7 Alexander MacDavid GUNN. The invented generation 4 Alexander would been born around 1480, about ninety years earlier than Barbara! Obviously that marriage did not happen.

Following on from that myth is another which says Barbara (with the invented 4. Alexander) had two sons with identical names alive at the same time – William Mhor and William Beag. That's wrong. The actual senior son of Alexander MacDavid Gunn and Barbara Mackay was William Mhor who had to be born around 1590, or perhaps a bit later. William Beag was the younger brother of Alexander MacDavid Gunn and therefore Uncle to William Mhor.

The proof for this is simple – firstly it is ridiculous to think there would be two siblings with identical names alive at the one time. Nobody has that in a family.

More importantly it's historically impossible. Barbara was definitely born around 1570 so her son William Mohr cannot be more than about eleven years old in about 1600. But there is a 'William MacHamish Gunn of[8] Killernan' in the historic records doing serious fighting on the Isle of Lewis at that time!

The 'William MacHamish Gunn of Killernan' doing that fighting cannot be William Mhor – it has to be another 'William MacHamish Gunn Killernan' from an earlier generation. Having two MacHamishes of Killernan alive at the same time again shows that MacHamish was not a title for a single person which matched Chief of the Clan Gunn. The person doing the fighting on the Isle of Lewis was William Beag whose life appears later.

There is record of an 'Alexander Gunn alias Jameson' being alive in November 1623 and an Alexander Davidson (MacDavid) being in Sutherland in 1624; both suggest Alexander MacDavid was alive in 1624.

I suspect Alexander MacDavid Gunn's son William Mhor inherited the Killernan estate in 1624 but a legal document - no longer able to be found - says William Mhor inherited Killernan in 1614. I think 1614 was a misreading of a scrawled date on the outside of a legal document (as no details exist about the document's content) and that the year was 1624. This is the presumed date of death for Alexander MacDavid Gunn.

---

[8] The usage 'of' is an error which is discussed in his life.

8. William Mhor GUNN

Alexander MacDavid Gunn had a son William Mhor Gunn in the 1590s; interestingly 1590 is the date attached to him in an important 1896 Gunn family tree.

There is a problem with William Mhor in that many events attached to his life were actually part of his energetic Uncle William Beag's life – consider the earlier discussion about the Isle of Lewis.

A William MacHamish of Killernan was deeply involved - with many others - in a 1623 battle against the Earl of Caithness. There were other Gunns involved in the battle but they were not led by this William MacHamish: as often said MacHamish Gunns were not Chiefs who led clansmen. It is not clear if it was William Mhor doing the fighting but 1623 was also getting a bit late for William Beag to be involved, although fighting was certainly in William Beag's line.

Once one removes the stories which better fit William Beag then William Mhor fades into obscurity - we know his parents, he may have been involved in a battle in 1623 and he probably inherited Killernan in 1624.

There is no record of a marriage nor children. He was the end of a line. He died no later than 1635 as William Beag's eldest son[9] generation **8. Alexander of Killernan and of Navidale GUNN** took over Killernan before 1636.

---

[9] As said, William Beag was uncle to William Mohr.

5b. Senior MacHamish Gunns / 'Clan Gunn Chiefs' from William Beag

The descendants of generation 7. William Beag Gunn became the Senior MacHamish Gunn / Clan Gunn Chief following the death of his nephew generation 8. William Mhor.

*****

The Senior MacHamish line from 7. William Beag

7. William Beag GUNN (c. 1561-).
    8. **Alexander Killernan GUNN** (c. 1590-c. 1657). Sp. Mary Christiane (Dame) (Lady Fowlis) MACKAY (c. 1598-c. 1657).
        9. **John Killernan GUNN** (c. 1636-). Sp. Katherine (Christina?) SINCLAIR (c. 1640-).
            10. Alexander GUNN (c. 1658-). *He had two younger brothers. It is possible that Alexander was the Senior MacHamish at one point.*
        9. Alexander GUNN (c. 1638-). *Was he ever the Senior MacHamish? Possibly. Married well but with no known children.* Sp. Christina MACKAY.
        9. **Donald Crotach GUNN** (c. 1642-c. 1708). Sp. Margaret SUTHERLAND. *It is probable but not definite that Donald was a Senior MacHamish.*

26

10. Alexander of Badanloch later of Wester Helmsdale GUNN (c. 1681-c. 1763).

  11. William GUNN (c. 1755-1780).

  11. Morrison GUNN (c. 1760-).

10. George Corrish GUNN (1682-).

10. Esther GUNN (1685-).

10. William (Lt. Col.) GUNN (c. 1686-).

10. *Margaret GUNN* (c. 1708-). *From whom comes the senior known living MacHamish line with continual Gunn named descendants.* Spouse 11 John GUNN of Kinbrace Farm and elsewhere. His father was George Gunn of Borrobol – as such, John was a MacHeorish – son of George - Gunn.

  11. George Gunn Dalfridh / Achscoriclate whose line dies out of male Gunns. This line was recognised as Chief of the Clan by some in the 1800s

  11. Alexander Gunn of Dalnaglaton, second son. Sp. Janet / Jean MacLeod of Dalnaha.

  12. John Gunn Dalnaglaton and Baehour. Sp Mary Dunbar of Rowens.

  13 Donald Gunn (sennachie) 1765 – 1861. Braehour and Brawlbin. Sp. Catherine Gunn of Osclay (descended from the Gunns of Kinbrace)

This line can be further traced. In 1975 the most senior Gunn from this line was my father Jack Alexander Gunn.

27

Biographies of the Senior MacHamish Gunns From William Beag

7. William Beag GUNN

William Beag Gunn (born about 1560) was, as already mentioned, brother to **7. Alexander MacDavid GUNN**. Alexander was the senior MacHamish Gunn, William Beag was not. It is William's children who become the Senior MacHamish line after the death of Alexander MacDavid's son **8. William Mhor GUNN**.

William Beag is not recorded as being 'of Killernan' in documents of the time but his sons were so recorded – as already said, the 'of' indicates the renter ('owner') of a place. This suggests that when **8. William Mhor GUNN** died it was either after William Beag's death, or William Beag was too frail and so let his eldest son have the Killernan Estate.

William was a 'soldier / adventurer' who probably fought in Caithness in 1589 and 1601 (and perhaps elsewhere) and certainly fought in the real nastiness on the Isle of Lewis (1600 / 1601) – one view has the Isle of Lewis events as 'genocide.' He always fought for the Earl of Sutherland. This Earl probably visited William at Killernan in February 1602. William may have become a 'soldier / adventurer' due to his brother being senior to him and so having the Killernan Estate whereas William needed to make his fortune.

William Beag is involved in a violent criminal event in October 1617. He attacked James Ross, the third son of the Laird of Balmucky, with the help of his eldest son **8. Alexander Killernan GUNN**, and others. In 1620 (recorded in 1624) this **8. Alexander Killernan GUNN** (called 'Alexander MacHamish' in the 1624 document) and his younger brother 8. John in Navidale of Borrobol GUNN (called 'John MacHamish') physically abuse a person and steal all his goods.

The years 1617 and 1620 mean it is impossible for **8. Alexander Killernan GUNN** to be a son of **8. William Mhor GUNN** as 'Clan Gunn' myths presume. As already discussed **8. William Mhor GUNN** had to be born in the 1590s so having adult sons by 1617 is impossible.

It is noteworthy that **8. Alexander Killernan GUNN** and his brother 8. John in Navidale of Borrobol GUNN are identified as MacHamish at the same time so it is further proof that MacHamish is not a title held by one person but rather a name for members of a family group.

William Beag Gunn had four known sons –

1.   **(Generation 8) Alexander Killernan Gunn**
2.   John in Navidale of Borrobol Gunn, alive 1652. He had a son, George Gunn of Borrobol. The Borrobol Estate seems to be for many years 'owned' by the next in line to the Senior MacHamish Gunn of Killernan. AS said. the 19th Century Chiefs of the Clan Gunn come from this line. Descendants are known.
3.   Donald the Scholar of Kinbrace Gunn from whom descendants are known.
4.   William of Acheneccan Gunn. Probable descendants.

8. Alexander of Killernan and of Navidale GUNN

Alexander of Killernan and of Navidale was born around 1590. As already mentioned, in 1617 and 1620 he participated in violent, criminal attacks.

Marriage.

Alexander married once and married well – he was the second husband of the independently wealthy Dame Mary Lady Foulis (originally Mackay) whose first husband died in April 1635. She initially married in 1619 so was not young when she had children with Alexander. (Various MacHamish Gunns and Mackays marry over the years which has been the source of much confusion.)

In 1636, the year after his marriage, Alexander Gunn 'of Killernan' is mentioned in a document 'renting' Navidale as well as keeping the Killernan Estate – did his marriage enable this? Alexander, obviously, inherited Killernan before 1636.

Alexander became of importance – he was in an August 1643 Act of Parliament and one of 1649 both being about Sutherland Committees. A 1652 Sutherland Estate document lists 'Alexander Gunn of Killernan' and his brother John who was 'of Borboll.' This document lists the land of the Killernan Estate, which included Killernan, Borrobol, Learable and Auld Breakachie. Learable is of interest as Learable Gunns are mentioned fairly often in various Sutherland papers - I suspect they are a branch of MacHamish Gunns but how they fit into the MacHamish story is not clear.

Alexander died by May 1658.

The children of Alexander Gunn were

- 1. **John of Killernan and Navidale GUNN**

- 2. Catherine Gunn. She married Aeneas / Angus
  Mackay the second son of Lord Reay. Descendants
  are known.

- 3. Alexander Gunn. He married well to Christina /
  Christina Mackay, some time before 1668. They
  probably lived at Navidale. It is likely that
  Alexander tried to buy Killernan from his brother in
  1668 perhaps using money from his wife's dowry
  but the transfer of ownership did not happen at that
  time. It may have happened later - the ownership of
  Killernan between 1679 and 1704 is unclear.
  Alexander is recorded as a spendthrift and
  'maintained great state (and) seldom moved without
  a great 'tail.'' Issue is recorded for this marriage but
  if such existed the children have disappeared from
  history. There is a Gunn story which talks about the
  murder of some MacHamish Gunns – such an event
  would explain the disappearance of these children.
  Overall, it is not clear whether this Alexander Gunn
  was ever the Senior MacHamish - he may have
  been, but on balance I think was not.

- 4. **Donald Crotach GUNN** who is the next known
  probable Senior MacHamish Gunn after his eldest
  brother John. He is discussed after his brother
  John's life.

9. John GUNN of Killernan and of Navidale

John was born around 1638. He married Catherine Sinclair who had a marriage dowry of 4,000 merks. John bankrupted Killernan and Navidale and 'Balnavaliache.' His debt in 1670 was approximately £2400 Scots which included 2,000 Scots merks to his first cousin George Gunn of Borrobol from whom came the MacHeorish Gunns. It is a lot of money – the Navidale Estate was gained on wadset for £800 Scots in 1636 so John owed the equivalent of something like two to three large Estates! The money owed was not helped by the 'total failure of the crops' which is mentioned in a 1679 document.

That document also mentions John had three sons, Alexander and two unnamed others. It also described this Alexander as 'of Killernan' (and therefore the Senior MacHamish) at one point but at another, confusingly, it was John who was still 'of Killernan.' It is possible that Alexander took over at Killernan and John moved to Navidale; was Navidale a retirement Estate?

The three sons after mention in that document disappear from history. Descent from them would be possible – and such descent would certainly be the Senior MacHamish line. As already mentioned, there is a Gunn story about the murder of some MacHamish Gunns – such an event would explain why this line disappeared, but so would a lack of money after losing Killernan.

MacHamish Gunns lose Killernan sometime between 1679 and 1704. There is a fanciful story (a plot involving a fire of legal papers!) to explain this loss but the prosaic truth is that the Gunns went bankrupt and returned Killernan to the Sutherland Estate.

9. Donald Crotach GUNN in Killernan of Badanloch

Donald was the youngest son of **8. Alexander of Killernan and of Navidale GUNN** and youngest brother of **9. John GUNN of Killernan and of Navidale**. He was a 'crotach' – a hunchback.

I am treating Donald Crotach Gunn as a Senior MacHamish but that could be wrong. To restate – Donald's eldest brother **9. John GUNN of Killernan and of Navidale** was the Senior MacHamish in 1679. John had three sons - Alexander and two others. Alexander was at one point possibly 'of Killernan' which suggests he was the Senior MacHamish. Alexander and his brothers disappear from history but descendants could exist. In other words, Donald and his children may not be Senior MacHamishes.

Donald was born no later than 1647 when his mother was around forty-seven. He was still living in Killernan in 1668 but was tacksman / wadset holder (the person who rented) 'of' Badanloch in Sutherland by 1704 where he was also a 'Commissioner of Supply' – a tax raiser, a position of some importance. Donald was certainly dead by 1709 as his eldest son had taken over at Badanloch by then.

The death year 1709 is important – one Gunn myth has Donald 'raising the Gunns' for the Jacobites in 1715. That is obviously wrong as he was dead! And there are no historic records of Gunns being involved with supporting the Jacobites at any time. Why would they? The land they wadsetted was owned by Protestants, the Gunns were Protestants, the Scottish Highlands were Protestant and Jacobites were Catholic. Donald's eldest son Alexander did turn out in 1745 on the side of the Government. More on that in his life.

Badanloch is further inland than Killernan but it was closer to other members of his extended family who held various estates near Badanloch. This might help explain why Donald moved from Killernan. Donald's son Alexander paid the 'entry bond' on the property in a mix of cash and cows over a period of years.

Donald married Margaret Sutherland of Torbal / Torroble / Torboll. They had five known children (probably more, given the time) and, bar for the first, we do not know their sequence.

The children, and probable sequence, were –

- 1. **Alexander GUNN of Badanloch** later Wester Helmsdale.

- 2. George 'Corrish' Gunn. George had two sons with no issue. The line is extinct.

- 3. Esther Gunn. She married Donald Mackay of Skerray, descendants.

- 4. William Gunn c. 1695 – 1768. Netherlands. Descendants, but not named Gunn, are known.

- 5. **Margaret GUNN.** In 2023 the most senior MacHamish Gunns known to have always had the surname Gunn - the traditional Clan Gunn Chief line if you like – are her descendants, namely from the Braehour Gunns. In other words, this line provides the ongoing traditional Clan Gunn Chief line.

10. Alexander GUNN of Badanloch, later Wester Helmsdale.

Alexander was probably born around 1683 and died in 1763. He used the surname 'Gun' when signing documents.

He was 'of' Badanloch by January 1709 – the Head of the MacHamish family. He never referred to himself as 'Chief of the Clan Gun' even when it would have been appropriate to do so in many legal documents – which he wrote - again showing Gunns never had Clan Chiefs.

Alexander's first wife was Margaret / Mary Mackay of Kirtomy. They married in 1721 and had four children. One of these children (Mary / Margaret) married Major Hugh Mackay of Rearquhar in July 1837, and had a child who died young. No other descendants are known for her. The other three children of Alexander's first marriage either died young or died without descendants.

Alexander was a spendthrift. Various stories attached to him suggest so – one phrasing is that he lived in 'considerable style and pomp'.

Alexander acquired Wester Helmsdale on 31 October 1718 for 4000 Scottish merks. How did he go from paying for Badanloch by cows and cash in 1709 to having a spare 4000 merks a bare nine years later? Simple. He was a ruthless landlord which is made clear in the 1738 documents discussed next.

Legal problems

There is a Clan Gunn fantasy that Alexander was some sort of legal genius. That does not match the facts.

There are massive amounts of legal documents for the year 1738 (at least forty-six large pages) in the Sutherland Estate papers in the National Library of Scotland concerning Alexander Gunn and the battles he had with that Estate.

The documents include claim, counter claim and evidence. It involved legal arbiters, judicial review, interviews with the Badanloch tenants and summons to appear in Edinburgh at the 'Lords of Council' – the supreme court of Scotland.

The case basically was that in September 1720 Alexander renewed the Badanloch Estate at markedly under market rate from an underage Earl of Sutherland, that Alexander did not pay the debts he owed the Sutherland Estate (the 1738 figure owed was £6750 Scots – the 1708 wadset for Wester Helmsdale was about £2650 Scots so Alexander owed the equivalent of more than two large Estates!) and that Alexander did not make all the improvements which he claimed to have done on the Badanloch Estate.

Alexander lived at Wester Helmsdale by 1738. He had sublet part (all?) of the Badanloch Estate to his father-in-law for more than Alexander was charged by the Sutherland Estate for Badanloch! Alexander also received money from the tenant farmers on Badanloch. The 1738 documents also detail how much Wester Helmsdale Estate deteriorated once Alexander had acquired it.

There is no legal document known indicating the result of the legal battle but the result is obvious. By the time of his second wife's second marriage there was no money to support the two sons Alexander had with her. Neither of those sons lived on an Estate as an adult - both held lowly positions in the military. In other words, his legal battle with the Sutherland Estate was comprehensively lost and the Estate and money was gone.

Second marriage

Alexander's second wife was Anne / Ann Rose (1733 - 1793) – remember Alexander was born around 1682 so that is about a fifty-year age gap between his wife and him. Why did she marry someone so much older than herself especially as Alexander had lost the legal battle with the Sutherland estate so was not a prize catch? I cannot find her marriage date nor the birthdate of her first son...

They had two children – **11. William GUNN** who would have been born no later than 1759 and his younger brother 11. Morrison Gunn. They are further discussed in their lives which follow this one.

After Alexander's death in 1763 Anne / Ann married again and had two children (David and Catherine) with Mr John Ross, Minister of Kildonan. Catherine married David Gunn of the MacHamish Acheneccan Gunn line, this being the descent line from the fourth son of William Beag. It is recorded that in this second marriage Anne / Ann was 'extravagant' and 'nearly ruined' her husband.

Alexander's military 'career'

Alexander's military 'career' needs rethinking; he is often referred to as Captain Alexander Gunn of Badanloch. That's pushing it.

Alexander was certainly Captain of the Clan Sutherland Independent 1st Company at Inverness in 1745. This Independent Company was formed to help put down the Jacobites; these independent companies were normally drawn from a Clan but in Alexander Gunn's case the Company was drawn from Clan Sutherland. In the list of officers of all the Independent Companies of Scotland raised in 1745 (meaning Captains, Lieutenants and Ensigns) there was only one Gun(n) and it's him - *'Alexander Gun, Esq.'*

This 1st Company was involved at the Siege of Fort Augustus in December 1745 and may have fought at the skirmish of Tongue but I suspect neither involved Alexander Gunn as he is not listed in those who received prizemoney which would be expected as he was Captain. By June 1746 the role of the companies had been markedly reduced and by October 1746 the companies were disbanded.

Alexander's military activity therefore seems to have lasted, at most, eleven months. His age needs to be considered – he was probably born about 1683 so he would be about 63 years old when the action occurred so lack of participation is understandable.

I would suggest, paying attention to a document in the legal battle of 1738, that Alexander Gunn may have been forced to turn out for Clan Sutherland or lose Wester Helmsdale as that document said there was an *'express clause in the Tack oblidgeing Mr Gun to wait on the said Noble Lord ... weapon shewings well armed when ... required by the said noble Lord.'*

So, the idea held by some that Alexander Gunn's brief military duty was some sort of 'Clan Gunn' obligation does not match the facts.

Overall, there is little to commend Alexander Gunn of Badanloch, later Wester Helmsdale.

11. William GUNN and his brother 11. Morrison Gunn

William Gunn was born circa 1757 and died at Conjeveram, Mysore (now Tamil Nadu), India, on 10 September 1780.

We do not know William's exact birthdate although his military enrolment document might show it if it could be found. William joined (most likely through a bought commission) the First Battalion of the 73rd (Highland) Regiment of Foot (MacLeod's Highlanders) as a lieutenant. It was raised in December 1777.

The First Battalion landed at Madras 20 January 1780. *'Of the 19 lieutenants of the 1st battalion* (of the 73rd Regiment)*, William Gunn stood 15th... six feet three'*. William Gunn died in the Battle of Pollilur of the Second Anglo-Mysore War of 1779-1784. It was a battle of importance;

After the treaty of Paris in 1763, the only serious
political threats to the British in the Madras area came
from Hyder Ali and his son Tipu Sultan. During the war
of 1780, the prowess of Hyder Ali and his cavalry
sometimes greatly intimidated the British. In no situation
was this more apparent than during the battle of
Pullalur, an area about ten miles north of Kanchipuram
to the west of Madras. This battle was fought by a British
force under the command of Colonel John Baillie
against those of Hyder Ali and Tipu on 10 September
1780, shortly after the beginning of the war. Various
mistakes made by the British commander-in-chief Sir
Hector Munro and by Baillie himself resulted in the
isolation of Baillie's force. Hyder Ali and Tipu, aided by
the French, soundly defeated Baillie's forces: of the
eighty-six officers in Baillie's force who participated,
thirty-six were killed or died of their wounds, thirty-four
were wounded and taken prisoner, and sixteen were
unwounded but taken prisoner.

Though the military encounter was brief, it had
great consequences for the fortunes and self-esteem of
the British at the time and long afterwards. Moreover,
because the defeat placed in doubt the British ability to
defend Madras, Hyder's rout of Baillie greatly
decreased British political and economic credibility...[10]

In other words, William Gunn was killed in a battle
which the British lost, to a significant extent because of
British mistakes. He was unfortunate; out of the British

---

[10]http://publishing.cdlib.org/ucpressebooks/view?docId=ft038n99hg&chunk.id
=s1.1.2&toc.id=ch01&brand=ucpress accessed 27 March 2013.

force of 3,820 only 336 were killed.[11] The final result of this war was the East India Company was told by the British government to make peace with the Kingdom of Mysore and basically the status quo resumed.

The official view of the battle involving William Gunn is simple –

Upon this unfortunate occasion, the flank companies were almost annihilated. Capt. Baird received seven wounds, and fell into the hands of the enemy. Lieut. Lindsay received nine and was also made prisoner. Lieut. Lindsay was totally disabled by his wounds; and Lieut. Gunn, of the grenadiers, and Lieut. Geddes Mackenzie, of the light company, killed, being the sum total of the officers serving at the time with the two companies. ... The melancholy fate of these companies rendered it necessary for Lord M'Leod to form two new flank companies from the battalion.[12]

There is another 'Clan Gunn' myth concerning William's brother Morrison. He was supposed to have joined the Second Battalion of the then 73rd Regiment - Lord Macleod's Highlanders – probably on the basis that his brother joined the First Battalion and it is also supposed that Morrison died at Gibraltar[13] whilst part of that Second Battalion. These suppositions seem to originate from this story –

---

[11] Figures from http://en.wikipedia.org/wiki/Second_Anglo-Mysore_War accessed 27 March 2013.
[12] Page 278, *The United Services Journal and Naval and Military Magazine, 1831, Part III.*
[13] The Great Siege of Gibraltar lasted 24 June 1779 – 7 February 1783.

'Morrison died of consumption, immediately after the siege of Gibraltar which he went through. He was most anxious to return to his native land as soon as the fortress was relieved, but his Colonel seeing that he had only a few days to live refused leave… The 2nd (Battalion) *came home from Gibraltar in 1783….* [14]

The Gibraltar story is wrong -

• There is a record of the officers of the Second Battalion of the 73rd Regiment and Morrison Gunn is not on the roll as an officer. If you are not on military records you were not part of the military - the army does not make mistakes in something as basic as the official roll. His brother William was certainly in the First Battalion; he is on the rolls as a Lieutenant.

• There is a range of primary sources from the Gibraltar siege detailing life, deaths and injuries sustained by many, including the soldiers. I have not found any mention of Morrison Gunn.

• The idea of a Commander being concerned with leave in 1783 from siege worn Gibraltar is odd; I doubt there would have been any chance of leave from such a place as the Battalion was getting ready to return to Britain. Gibraltar was not a holiday spot with regular transport for occasional military personnel.

What is known is that a Morrison Gunn was gazetted as a lieutenant from the war-office on 24 July 1779 to the Sutherland Fencibles. The Fencibles were recruited from

---

[14] http://clangunn.weebly.com/thomas-sinclair-supplement-4-23-12-1902.html accessed 2 April 2018.

the Sutherland Estate where Morrison lived. It was officially formed at Fort George (near Inverness) in February 1779 and then served at Edinburgh. Recruiting originally went poorly; but then *'the promise of land in return for service'* was offered. This land offer may well have motivated Morrison to enlist. The Regiment was disbanded in 1783. It was a sort of home guard.

I suspect this Sutherland Fencibles lieutenant was Morrison Gunn. Morrison had the example of his older brother joining the real army (an expensive occupation which probably took the last of the Gunn money) and Morrison needed a job as the family no longer owned an Estate. As well, the Sutherland Fencibles story makes sense with the *'refused leave'* - you could get leave from Edinburgh or Inverness far more reasonably than from war-torn, isolated Gibraltar. Also, this was the second incarnation of the Sutherland Fencibles, so supporting the use of '2nd' in the original story. It is to be regretted that the records of the Fencibles are minimal.

It is most likely that Morrison died from consumption (given the unglamorous death I suspect it had a real origin) sometime after being commissioned. Given William died 10 September 1780 it is not clear that Morrison was ever the Senior of the MacHamish line. With the deaths of the two brothers[15] the Senior MacHamish Gunn line was lost in confusion for years.

---

[15] Lord Lyon provides a date of 1 May 1785 for Morrison's death; this is wrong. If the Gibraltar story had been true then Morrison needed to die before May 1783 when his battalion returned from Gibraltar. http://www.lyon-court.com/lordlyon/files/Gunn,%20Michael%20James%20-%20Interlocutor%20and%20Note.pdf accessed 1 April 2018.

6. The Clearances

The Highland Clearances of 1790-1855 have been extremely well covered by historians over many years and those wishing for the full detail should explore their texts. Simplistically the key question is 'Were the Clearances 'ethnic cleansing' (*'sheep before people!'*) or has the process merely had a bad press?'

The answer is that it was something in between.

The Clearances (which involved much more than just Gunn rented lands) are best viewed as legal, Victorian, well-meaning paternalistic actions by landowners, but these actions were occasionally forceful or violent.

The Sutherland Estate got involved with the Clearances for two reasons – the first was the Estate would be more productive with sheep rather than tenant farmers but the second reason was that with the extra money earned a significant amount would go to improve the lives of the tenants.[16]

In other words, sheep would pay for improvements on the Estate which would include helping the *'common people.'*

What this ideal meant in practice on the Sutherland Estate around 1820 was –

• The Sutherland Estate tenants had notice in November 1817 that they would be moved starting May

---

[16] Pages 156-157, Eric Richards *The Highland Clearances*.

1819. The last year on their old land would be rent free and arrears of rent were ignored. That's a lot of rent which would not go to the Sutherland Estate!

- This information was regularly repeated, including by local Ministers and personal communication. So, all tenants would know what was happening and when.

- Tenants were offered replacement lots at Helmsdale of between one or two Scots acres, or at Brora with lots of two acres with land already ploughed and ready for cultivation. Coastal allotments for the first year were rent free (remember these tenants already had a free year before moving). For those who thought such land too small six to twelve acres were offered on Dornoch Moors and Five Pounds was given for every acre brought into cultivation. In other words, tenants had generous bonuses when they moved from their old land.

- This long advance warning before moving meant tenants could build new homes before they had to leave their old houses. (Tenants were always responsible for the homes in which they lived – it was never an Estate responsibility. And Estate timber was provided for these new homes free of charge.)

- With regard to the burning of tenants' houses a report of the time[17] said -

---

[17] From the Sutherland Estate papers, National Library of Scotland, especially 'Extracts from letters received by Mr Sutherland from persons resident in the North respecting the practice of "Burning out the Tenants on the Estate of Sutherland". They were in a letter addressed to J. Lock / Loch Esq, posted 18 July 1819 in Bloomsbury, London.

The account of being burnt out of their huts is equally untrue, in those instances indeed where the tenant either did not, or from the distant situation of his hut, could not carry away the timber, it was burnt, but not until after valuation of two sworn appraisers, in order to prevent them being reoccupied ... and ... *there was not a House in which the least symptom of sickness appeared but was left undisturbed and the inhabitants allowed to remain in quiet possession.*

In other words, the tenants' houses were owned by them and they were expected to remove these houses from their old rented land before they moved to new homes for which the Estate had given them free timber. If the tenants could not move the old homes for some reason the houses were valued by independent valuers, the money given to the tenants and then – only then – was the house burned so the old homes could not be squatted in. These moving arrangements went on from 1807 until at least 1820. The Clearances, overall, were not done in a rush.

• For the more criminally inclined tenant things were different. The previously mentioned report said -

It has been a rule upon this, as it is upon other Estates in the Country, to remove from their holdings all Offenders against the Law, upon their being convicted of Sheep stealing, Illegal Distillation, Destroying the woods, Killing the Fish in close time, or of any other depredation on the property of the Landlord or tacksman ... This rule was not abandoned on the present occasion, and persons actually convicted of these crimes before a

46

Magistrate, amounting in number to about one hundred, one half of whom were also heads of Families were not to be retained upon the estate.

So, overall, the Sutherland Estate Clearances should be seen as patronising with an 'Estate knows best' and 'don't be a nuisance in any way or the Estate will not give you anything' attitude – but it's certainly not the ethnic cleansing which so many think.

Contemplate the Clearances in a modern way - imagine living two years rent free. That just doesn't happen. But that is basically what the Sutherland Estate offered.

Yes, a few serious mistakes were made; for example, the Kildonan riots of 1813 were caused by too hastily requiring people to move but this haste was not deliberate policy, more inexperience. Mind you, at least one suggestion for the reluctance of the Kildonan people to move at that time *'was attributed to their whisky smuggling activities which were sure to be restricted'* when they settled elsewhere.

Migration? Sure, some happened, but migration started a long time before the Clearances - one estimate suggests Scottish migration of between 85,000 and 115,000 between 1600 and 1650.[18] In fact, very few people emigrated to America in response to the Clearances.[19]

---

[18] Page 5, T. M. Devine, *Scotland's Empire 1600-1815* Penguin, 2004.
[19] This is supported elsewhere; Page 36 David Forbes *The Sutherland Clearances 1806-1820; An Introduction* points out that only 83 people emigrated in 1819 whereas 2,304 were resettled on the Sutherland Estate and 889 settled elsewhere in Sutherland.

What the Sutherland Estate did was legal and evokes modern planning,[20] the actions were no worse than that done elsewhere and was done with an awareness of the need to improve the lives of the people on their estate.

And was it all as efficient / ruthless as many say? One view is *'the obstinate people* (Gunns) *of the Heights of Kildonan ... rapidly rebuilt their huts from their old timber ... they simply drove their cattle out of sight when the clearing parties approached and then returned the stock to their old pastures when the constables departed.'*[21]

One has to mention the Factor ('Overseer') of the Sutherland Estate at one time in the Clearances was (MacHamish Generation 13) George Gunn[22] who was 'Chief of the Clan Gunn' in some views; he certainly *'rearranged groups of tenantry in Kildonan and Loth at Rovie and Craigton.'*[23]

So, no matter your view of the Clearances the Gunn hierarchy was certainly partly responsible for it. Incidentally George Gunn was loathed by the earlier Factor on the Sutherland Estate, Patrick Sellar.

*****

---

[20] 'the Marquis of Stafford and his wife had been responsible for the kind of approach which foreshadowed modern regional planning'. Page 39, David Forbes *The Sutherland Clearances 1806-20; An Introduction.*

[21] Page 240, Eric Richards *Patrick Sellar and the Highland Clearances.*

[22] He was from the first son of Margaret Gunn (daughter of Chief Donald Crotach Gunn) and John Gunn MacHeorish of Kinbrace Farm). The line died out of male Gunns.

[23] Page 269, Eric Richards *Patrick Sellar and the Highland Clearances.*

One view of the Gunns of this time –

Clan Gunn

... (lived) in a most remote and inaccessible country, they continued to live in the committal of continued breaches of the law and yet to escape punishment. This character, even to a late day, distinguished in a remarkable manner, some individuals of this Clan and district, and the people of the heights of Kildonan were long noted for being the least observant of the laws of any in the county. Indeed it is only within the last five years that the disappearance of a sheriff's officer, who was sent up to execute a warrant in a civil process, led to the recollection of many stories of former days. Their country was peculiarly favourable for carrying on illegal distillation, and they did not neglect to take advantage of their situation. They obtained, with much ease, their grain from the corn districts of the adjoining county of Caithness, and the inaccessible and remote situations of their habitations, made it neither very easy nor advisable, for the revenue officers to follow them into their recesses. The nature of their country gave them equal facilities in disposing of their whiskey....

Being from pages 97-99 of *An account of the improvements on the estates of the Marquess of Stafford in the Counties of Stafford and Salop and on the Estate of Sutherland with Remarks* by James Loch Esquire, James Loch had been a Factor on the Sutherland Estate.

7. Finally

To restate, real Gunn history is a minor part of Scottish Highland history.

Coroner Gunn was the first Gunn known and he was of major importance. His eldest son's senior descent line - the MacHamish Gunns – can be readily traced today. I am one of them. The Coroner's second son's line can also be found. But these family lines are of little significance[24] unless you can trace your descent to them.

The Victorians, inspired by Sir Walter Scott, remade the history of the Highlands into a work of fiction and Gunn history was part of this reinvention. In consequence the commonly found 'Clan Gunn' history (which is not the same as real Gunn history) should be viewed as being as historically accurate as the Disney film 'Brave.'

In reality Gunns are an exclusive group – they have a regional name derived from the original people of northern mainland Scotland which is something of national significance.

Gunns should celebrate their name's origin and their own family, and not be bogged down in the trivia of 'Clan Gunn' fantasy, dress-up[25] 'history'.

*****

---

[24] If you believe in the myth of 'Clan Gunn Chiefs' then this means the 'Chief line is not extinct.

[25] Clan Gunn named tartan was invented in 1842 for the tourist market.

Brawlbin farm 2011.

Donald Gunn of Braehour and Brawlbin was the great-grandson of Margaret Gunn (daughter of Chief Donald Crotach Gunn) and John MacHeorish Gunn of Kinbrace Farm and elsewhere).
Donald's family provides the ongoing Clan Gunn Chief line.

Appendix: The Clan Gunn Chief line

The figures in brackets such as (1,1) give the MacHamish identification; the first number shows the generation, the second the seniority of that MacHamish.. Those who die without issue only have a generation number. The name in **bold** is the Senior MacHamish at some point, see page 18.

Generation		
1	**Coroner Gunn** (1,1)	
2	**James Gunn** (2,2)	
3	**William MacHamish 'Cattaig' Gunn** (3,3)	
4	**William MacHamish Gunn** (4,4)	
5	**Unknown MacHamish Gunn** (5,5)	
6	**David MacHamish Gunn** (6,6) 1st son, with son Alexander MacDavid Gunn (7,7) who had William Mohr (8,) who died without known issue.	
6	William 'Beag' Gunn (6,8) 2nd son	
8	**Alexander Killernan Gunn** (8,9) 1st son	John Gunn in Navidale of Borrobol (8,10) 2nd son

9	**Donald Crotach Gunn** (9,15) 3rd son	George Borrobol Gunn (9,16)
10	**Margaret Gunn** (10, 23) *married John Gunn of Kinbrace Farm, Grimachary (10,24)* ←→	John Gunn *of Kinbrace Farm, Grimachary (10,24)*
11	Alexander Gunn of Dalnaglaton 2nd son.[26]	
12	John Gunn, Dalnaglaton and Braehour	
13	Donald Braehour and Brawlbin Gunn *married Catherine Osclay Gunn. This line has the continuing traditional Clan Gunn Chief line.*	

---

[26] *The line of the 1st son ran out of Gunns in 1975.*

Milton Keynes UK
Ingram Content Group UK Ltd.
UKHW050836141123
432524UK00001B/2